# FASAB

Federal Accounting Standards Advisory Board

# Overview of Federal Accounting Concepts and Standards
(as of September 30, 1996)

## Reporting Relevant Financial Information

Report Number 1

*December 31, 1996*

December 31, 1996

We have prepared this overview to help agency managers and other interested parties understand the kinds of financial information that will be available under new reporting concepts and accounting standards developed by the Federal Accounting Standards Advisory Board (FASAB).

FASAB was established in October 1990 by the Secretary of the Treasury, the Director of the Office of Management and Budget (OMB), and the Comptroller General to consider and recommend accounting principles for the federal government. The nine member Board is composed of representatives from the three principals, one Congressional Budget Office representative, one representative from the defense and international agencies, one representative from civilian agencies, and three representatives from the private sector.

FASAB recommends accounting standards after considering the financial and budgetary information needs of the Congress, executive agencies, other users of federal financial information, and comments from the public. Treasury, OMB, and the General Accounting Office (GAO) then decide whether to adopt the recommended standards; if they do, the standards are published by OMB and GAO and become effective.

Using a due process and consensus building approach, the Board and the FASAB staff have provided the federal government with a set of comprehensive accounting standards. The dedication of all FASAB members and staff has contributed greatly to this landmark achievement and we commend the important contribution they have made to improve federal accounting and financial reporting.

The new reporting concepts and accounting standards that have resulted are central to effectively meeting the financial management improvement goals of the Chief Financial Officers (CFO) Act of 1990, as amended. Also, improved financial information is necessary to support the strategic planning and performance measurement requirements of the Government Performance and Results Act (GPRA) of 1993.

The preface highlights the objectives of federal financial reporting and the financial information to be reported by federal agencies. Subsequent sections summarize each of the statements of reporting concepts and accounting standards issued to date. These sections are organized as follows. The first three sections present FASAB's overall financial reporting conceptual framework, with the third section also covering managerial cost accounting standards. Next, accounting for the federal government's revenue and other financing sources is discussed, followed by several sections covering accounting for its assets and liabilities. The final section addresses reporting on the federal government's investments in certain property, plant and equipment, human capital, research and development, and non-federal physical property acquired by grants to states and local governments.

The summaries of the concepts and standards provided in this document should not be used as a substitute for the actual statements of federal financial reporting concepts or accounting standards. The detailed standards are available from the Government Printing Office and on the Internet through FinanceNet. Also, FASAB will issue a codification of these concepts and standards. These standards have various implementation dates through fiscal year 1998; the standards may be amended in the future as necessary and additional standards are expected to be issued.

Elmer B. Staats
Chairman

# Preface

The reporting concepts and accounting standards described in this preface will provide new information on the federal government's financial condition, as well as on the costs of its programs. With this financial information, the Congress and government leaders will have relevant data to help make decisions affecting the budget, control costs, and measure performance. As a result, government programs can be managed more effectively, greater accountability for program results can be provided, and many future problems can be anticipated before they become crises.

The financial accounting standards adopted differ from those used in budgetary accounting to the extent necessary to meet the objectives of federal financial reporting in *Statement of Federal Financial Accounting Concepts Number 1*. For example, to help ensure that meaningful and reliable financial information is available to government decision-makers and the public, the standards developed by FASAB for the federal government are based on the accrual basis of accounting, which reports the substance of events when they occur.

The accounting standards developed by FASAB are tailored to the federal government's unique characteristics and special needs. For example, the federal government needs financial information that is useful in planning future budgets and in controlling budgetary expenditures; consequently net costs, rather than profit, is used as the major economic indicator of efficiency and effectiveness.

## Financial Reporting Objectives

Financial reporting objectives pertain to the purpose to be served by financial information. Federal agencies should provide information about:

- *budgetary integrity.* What legal authority was provided for financing government activities and for spending the monies? Were the financing and spending in accordance with these authorizations? How much (in terms of budgetary resources) is left?

- *operating performance.* How much do programs cost and how were they financed? What outputs and outcomes were achieved? What and where are the important assets, and how effectively are they managed? What liabilities arose from operating the programs, and how will they be liquidated or provided for?

---

Federal Accounting Standards Advisory Board
Federal Accounting Concepts and Standards
December 31, 1996

- *stewardship.* [NOTE 1: In the context of *Statement of Federal Financial Accounting Concepts Number 1, Objectives of Federal Financial Reporting*, the term stewardship broadly refers to the federal government's responsibility to be accountable for all of its operations and assessing the results based on an array of information to be presented in financial statements. As used in *Statement of Federal Financial Accounting Standards Number 8, Supplementary Stewardship Reporting*, the term stewardship is associated with a specific type of report that is to be included as part of an entity's financial statements and disclose information on its responsibility for such uniquely governmental assets as heritage assets, weapons systems, and space exploration equipment.] Did the government's financial condition improve or deteriorate? What provision has been made for the future?

- *controls.* Does the government have cost-effective systems and controls to safeguard its assets? Is it able to detect likely problems? Are deficiencies corrected when detected?

## Information To Be Reported

Using these objectives, FASAB has recommended and the three principals have adopted standards that prescribe the types of financial information federal entities should provide. OMB has incorporated the provisions of the standards in its guidance on the form and content of agency financial statements, issued pursuant to the CFO Act.

Financial information to be reported includes:

- *operating performance*: the total costs of agency and suborganization operations, revenues generated from operations used to fund costs, net cost of operations (cost of operations less revenues), and appropriations and taxes used to fund the net cost of operations;

- *budgetary information*: budgetary resources made available through appropriations and other sources, obligations incurred, outlays, and a reconciliation of obligations incurred to net cost of operations; and

- *financial status information*: unspent funds, operating assets (such as receivables and investment, property, plant, and equipment) and liabilities, including those related to credit and insurance programs and pensions and other postemployment benefits.

## Strengthening Accountability

The new reporting concepts and accounting standards, which are listed in appendix I, will provide comprehensive, understandable, and consistent information on the federal government's financial status. To help ensure the accuracy of this information, much of it will be audited, as required by the expanded CFO Act. Together, the new standards and financial audits will provide relevant and reliable financial information to strengthen accountability for government operations.

Federal Accounting Standards Advisory Board
Federal Accounting Concepts and Standards
December 31, 1996

# Contents

Preface .................................................................................................. 1

Objectives of Federal Financial Reporting ......................................... 7

Entity and Display ............................................................................... 11

Managerial Cost Accounting Concepts and Standards ..................... 15

Accounting for Revenue and Other Financing Sources ................... 19

Accounting for Selected Assets and Liabilities ................................. 25

Accounting for Property, Plant, and Equipment .............................. 29

Accounting for Inventory and Related Property .............................. 32

Accounting for Direct Loans and Loan Guarantees ........................ 36

Accounting for Liabilities .................................................................. 38

Supplementary Stewardship Reporting ............................................. 41

Appendix I
Statements of Federal Financial Accounting Concepts
  and Standards and Their Effective Dates ..................................... 44

---

Federal Accounting Standards Advisory Board
Federal Accounting Concepts and Standards
December 31, 1996

Abbreviations
CFO          Chief Financial Officer
FASAB        Federal Accounting Standards Advisory Board
GAO          General Accounting Office
GPRA         Government Performance and Results Act of 1993
IRS          Internal Revenue Service
OMB          Office of Management and Budget
PP&E         Property, Plant, and Equipment
SFFAC  Statements of Federal Financial Accounting Concepts
SFFAS        Statements of Federal Financial Accounting Standards

# Objectives of Federal Financial Reporting

The federal government derives its just powers from the consent of the governed. It therefore has a special responsibility to report on its actions and the results of those actions. These reports must accurately reflect the distinctive nature of the federal government and must provide information useful to the citizens, their elected representatives, federal executives, and program managers.

Providing this information to the public, news media, and elected officials is an essential part of accountability in government. Providing this information to program managers, executives, and members of the Congress is essential to planning and conducting government functions economically, efficiently, and effectively for the benefit of society.

*Statement of Federal Financial Accounting Concepts Number 1, Objectives of Federal Financial Reporting*, provides a conceptual statement on the objectives of financial reporting by the federal government. The objectives of federal financial reporting are based on the needs of those who use the reports, as expressed by them in a series of focus groups FASAB conducted. The users of federal financial reports include citizens, the Congress, federal executives, and federal program managers. Users of federal financial information want information to help them assess how the government is doing, financially. Their interests define the four objectives of federal financial reporting summarized here.

The objectives apply to both internal and external financial reports. They are intended to improve the relevance, consistency, and quality of accounting and other data available for a wide variety of applications.

## Significance of Statement

This concepts statement provides the guidance necessary to ensure that all the accounting standards issued meet the needs of users of federal financial reports. The statement has focused FASAB's entire standard-setting process and led to *Statement of Federal Financial Accounting Concepts Number 2, Entity and Display*, in which financial reports dealing with budgetary integrity, operating performance, and stewardship were identified. Federal government reporting on systems and controls has been an OMB responsibility and FASAB has not addressed the need for comprehensive disclosure or made other recommendations relating to systems and controls.

---

Federal Accounting Standards Advisory Board
Federal Accounting Concepts and Standards
December 31, 1996

*Statement of Federal Financial Accounting Concepts Number 1* will continue to guide FASAB's work to ensure that future standards are consistent with those objectives and deal with the special circumstances of the federal government in a way that meets users' needs for information.

## Budgetary Integrity

Federal financial reporting should assist in fulfilling the government's duty to be publicly accountable for monies raised through taxes and other means and for their expenditure in accordance with the appropriations laws that establish the government's budget for a particular fiscal year and related laws and regulations. Federal financial reporting should provide information that helps the reader to determine

- how budgetary resources have been obtained and used and whether their acquisition and use were in accordance with the legal authorization,
- the status of budgetary resources, and
- how information on the use of budgetary resources relates to information on the costs of program operations and whether information on the status of budgetary resources is consistent with other accounting information on assets and liabilities.

## Operating Performance

Federal financial reporting should assist report users in evaluating the service efforts, costs, and accomplishments of the reporting entity; the manner in which these efforts and accomplishments have been financed; and the management of the entity's assets and liabilities. Federal financial reporting should provide information that helps the reader to determine

- the costs of providing specific activities and programs and the composition of and changes in these costs;
- the efforts and accomplishments associated with federal programs and the changes over time and in relation to costs; and
- the efficiency and effectiveness of the government's management of its assets and liabilities.

## Stewardship

Federal financial reporting should assist report users in assessing the impact on the nation of the government's operations and investments and how, as a result, the government's and the nation's financial condition have changed and may change in the future.

Federal financial reporting should provide information that helps the reader to determine whether

- the government's financial position improved or deteriorated,
- future budgetary resources will likely be sufficient to sustain public services and to meet obligations as they come due, and

- government operations have contributed to the nation's current and future well-being.

## Systems and Controls

Federal financial reporting should assist report users in understanding whether financial management systems and internal accounting and administrative controls are adequate to ensure that

- transactions are executed in accordance with budgetary and financial laws and other requirements, consistent with the purposes authorized, and recorded in accordance with federal accounting standards;

- assets are properly safeguarded to deter fraud, waste, and abuse; and

- performance measurement information is adequately supported.

Federal Accounting Standards Advisory Board
Federal Accounting Concepts and Standards
December 31, 1996

# Entity and Display

Financial reports communicate financial and related information about an entity. Financial reports should provide users with all the information that is relevant to a reporting entity, subject to cost and time constraints.

*Statement of Federal Financial Accounting Concepts Number 2, Entity and Display* (1) specifies the types of entities for which there ought to be financial reports, (2) establishes guidelines for defining the makeup of each type of reporting entity, (3) identifies types of financial reports for communicating the information for each type of reporting entity, and (4) suggests the types of information each type of report would convey.

The entity and display concepts presented do not preclude the specification of ad hoc or temporary reporting entities to meet the special reporting needs of users of federal agencies' financial information. Nor do they preclude a reporting entity from preparing special purpose financial reports to meet specific information needs.

## Significance of Statement

This concepts statement defines the entity that should prepare financial statements (reporting entity) by establishing criteria for identifying the components of the reporting entity. This helps ensure that agencies reflect in their financial statements all of their activities, including component units for which they are responsible.

The statement also provides model financial reports designed to provide information that supports the objectives of federal financial reporting in *Statement of Federal Financial Reporting Concepts Number 1*. These models should facilitate federal efforts to communicate relevant financial and programmatic information to the user community.

## Determining Reporting Entities

To be a reporting entity, an entity would need to meet all of the following criteria.

- There is a management responsible for controlling and deploying resources, producing outputs and outcomes, executing the budget or a portion thereof, and held accountable for the entity's performance.

- The entity's scope is such that its financial statements would provide a meaningful representation of operations and financial condition.

- There are likely to be users of the financial statements who are interested in and could use the information in the statements to help them make resource allocation and other decisions and hold the entity accountable for its deployment and use of resources.

The financial statements of a reporting entity may include financial data on significant organizations, budget accounts, and programs which are not conterminous. To help identify which component units should be included in any given reporting entity, a list of criteria is presented for consideration. If an entity is included in the federal budget section entitled, Federal Programs by Agency and Account, then it meets the conclusive criteria. In addition, the statement provides indicative criteria that should be considered for entities that do not meet the conclusive criteria.

The financial results of government corporations, which by law must follow private sector accounting standards when they report separately, should also reflect statements of federal financial accounting standards (SFFAS) when those results are included in a larger reporting entity that follows SFFAS. SFFAS do not apply to the Legislative and Judicial Branches of government. Also, government sponsored enterprises and the Federal Reserve are not federal reporting entities.

## Displaying Financial Information

Financial information is typically provided by or for a reporting entity through financial statements. Financial statements represent the principal means of communicating accounting information about an entity's resources, obligations, revenues, costs, etc. to those outside the entity. Financial statements and related reporting specified by the entity and display concepts statement include:

- **Management discussion and analysis**, which is designated to summarize and explain the most significant aspects of the entity's performance and its financial affairs.

- **Balance sheet**, which is designed to report on the operating assets and liabilities related to the delivery of goods and services by government reporting entities.

- **Statement of net costs**, which is designed to report the gross and net costs of providing government goods, services, and benefits and will help in assessing the cost of service efforts and accomplishments.

- **Statement of changes in net position**, which is designed to provide information on the changes in financial position from year to year and the causes of the changes.

- **Statement of custodial activities**, which is designed to report, for those entities whose primary mission is collecting taxes or other revenues, the sources and disposition of amounts collected and collectible.

- **Statement of budgetary resources**, which is designed to present information related to budgetary resources made available, the status of budgetary resources, and outlays.

- **Statement of program performance measures**, which is designated to present outputs and outcomes for each of the major programs operated by the reporting entity.

- **Statement of financing**, which is designed to explain the relationship of budgetary obligations to costs recorded in the financial statements. (This statement was not originally included in *Statement of Federal Financial Accounting Concepts Number 2*, but was added as a concept later.)

In addition, an entity's financial report would include required **supplementary stewardship information** presented in conjunction with the financial statements, as well as accompanying footnotes, other required supplemental information, and other accompanying information.

Federal Accounting Standards Advisory Board
Federal Accounting Concepts and Standards
December 31, 1996

# Managerial Cost Accounting Concepts and Standards

The cost of government is a concern to the public as well as to the federal government itself. Unlike private business, there is no "bottom line" or profit index to help measure public sector performance. However, government service efforts and accomplishments can be evaluated using both financial and non-financial measures, and "cost" is the focus for measuring the financial results of government programs. Good cost information is helpful to managers seeking to improve the efficiency and cost-effectiveness of the programs they operate. It can also be used as a basis to estimate future costs in preparing and reviewing budgets.

*Statement of Federal Financial Accounting Standards Number 4, Managerial Cost Accounting Concepts and Standards for the Federal Government*, contains cost accounting concepts and standards for determining the costs of an entity's activities, programs, and outputs.

"Cost" is the monetary value of resources used or sacrificed or liabilities incurred to achieve an objective, such as to acquire or produce a good or to perform an activity or service. Costs incurred may benefit current and future periods. In financial accounting and reporting, the costs that apply to an entity's operations for the current period are recognized as expenses of that period.

## Significance of Standard

The standards covered by this statement determine how the costs and outputs of programs should be defined for both reporting and managerial purposes. The standards reflect modern concepts on how best to assign costs to focal points for cost accounting, such as government programs. For various reasons, these standards differ to some extent from the rules established by the Cost Accounting Standards Board for reporting to the federal government by contractors and grantees.

The standards will help achieve important objectives such as those that follow.

- Providing program managers with relevant and reliable information relating cost to outputs. This cost information will assist them in improving operational economy and efficiency. Based on this information, program managers can respond to inquiries about the cost of the activities they manage.

- Providing relevant and reliable cost information to assist the Congress and the Executive Branch in making decisions about allocating federal resources, authorizing and modifying programs, and evaluating program performance.

- Ensuring consistency between costs reported in general purpose financial reports and costs reported to program managers. This includes standardizing terminology for managerial cost accounting to improve communication among federal organizations and users of cost information.

For financial reporting, the standard requires the use of "full costs." That is, all the costs that are attributable to a federal entity, its programs, or its outputs. For example, the costs of federal entities include the cost of federal employee pensions, including those amounts funded through the Office of Personnel Management, as well as other inter-entity costs identified by OMB which meet the recognition criteria for such costs. In addition, FASAB has a current project considering whether the definition of "full cost" should include imputed interest cost on the capital assets employed by the entity.

In the case of many federal entities, obtaining accurate cost information will require substantially improved cost accounting systems. When it becomes available, such information will be useful, for example

- as a basis for pricing government goods and services and determining subsidies, if any;

- in controlling and reducing costs; and

- to budget planners in the agencies and to OMB and the Congress in reviewing budgetary proposals.

Under certain circumstances, cost concepts other than full cost also may be useful in managerial decision-making. For example, differential costs or incremental costs may be useful in making decisions on whether to add or eliminate a service or a product.

When the Government Performance and Results Act of 1993 becomes fully effective, these managerial cost accounting standards will provide the basis for important cost information, such as the unit costs of outputs (or outcomes).

## Concepts

Managerial cost accounting should be a fundamental part of a financial management system and, to the extent practicable, should be integrated with other parts of the system. Managerial costing should use a basis of accounting, recognition, and measurement appropriate for the intended purpose. Cost information developed for different purposes should be drawn from a common data source, and output reports should be reconcilable to each other.

## Standards

There are five managerial cost accounting standards that set forth the fundamental elements of managerial cost accounting: (1) accumulating and reporting the costs of activities on a regular basis for management information purposes, (2) establishing responsibility segments to match costs with outputs, (3) determining the full costs of government goods and services, (4) recognizing the costs of goods and services received from other federal entities, and (5) using appropriate costing methodologies to accumulate and assign costs to outputs.

## Requirement for Cost Accounting

Each reporting entity should accumulate and report the costs of its activities on a regular basis for management information purposes. Costs may be accumulated either through the use of cost accounting systems or through the use of cost finding techniques.

## Responsibility Segments

The management of each reporting entity should define and establish responsibility segments. Managerial cost accounting should be performed to measure and report the costs of each segment's outputs. Special cost studies, if necessary, should be performed to determine the costs of outputs.

## Full Cost

Reporting entities should report the full costs of outputs in general purpose financial reports. The full cost of an output produced by a responsibility segment is the sum of (1) the costs of resources consumed by the segment that directly or indirectly contribute to the output, and (2) the costs of identifiable supporting services provided by other responsibility segments within the reporting entity and by other reporting entities.

## Inter-entity Costs

Each entity's full cost should incorporate the full costs of goods and services that it receives from other entities. The entity providing the goods or services has the responsibility to provide the receiving entity with information on the full costs of such goods or services either through billing or other advice.

Recognition of inter-entity costs that are not fully reimbursed is limited to material items that (1) are significant to the receiving entity, (2) form an integral or necessary part of the receiving entity's output, and (3) can be identified or matched to the receiving entity with reasonable precision. Broad and general support services provided by an entity to all or most other entities generally should not be recognized unless such services form a vital and integral part of the operations or output of the receiving entity.

## Costing Methodology

The costs of resources consumed by responsibility segments should be accumulated by type of resource. Outputs produced by responsibility segments should be accumulated and, if practicable, measured in units. The full costs of resources that directly or indirectly contribute to the production of outputs should be assigned to outputs through costing methodologies or cost finding techniques that are most appropriate to the segment's operating environment and should be followed consistently.

The cost assignments should be performed using the following methods listed in the order of preference: (a) directly tracing costs wherever feasible and economically practicable, (b) assigning costs on a cause-and-effect basis, or (c) allocating costs on a reasonable and consistent basis.

# Accounting for Revenue and Other Financing Sources

*Statement of Federal Financial Accounting Standards Number 7, Accounting for Revenue and Other Financing Sources*, provides standards for classifying, recognizing, and measuring all resource inflows and for relating those inflows to costs incurred by the entity. In addition, it deals with budgetary resources from a budgetary perspective and how these relate to costs incurred by the entity. The standard also provides important disclosures about the more than $1 trillion of federal taxes annually and prescribes special accounting and disclosure requirements for trust funds.

## Significance of Standard

This standard's treatment of exchange revenue and related accrual accounting requirements together with the requirements of the managerial cost accounting standards, provide the basis for determining the net cost of the programs and outputs of the reporting entity. With a few minor exceptions, the entity's net cost and the net cost of its programs represent costs borne by the taxpayer, making this data particularly relevant to those interested in knowing where taxpayer dollars are spent and with what result.

The standard recognizes the inherent and practical limitations on the ability of the collectors to measure revenue from taxes and duties as nonexchange revenue. This is compensated to the extent possible by supplemental information and other disclosures about the tax collection process.

This standard provides for the linking of the net cost of the entity to budget execution information through a reconciliation; thus the entity's cost data are more easily comprehensible to budget planners and the Congress.

In addition, this standard requires entities to provide information on amounts collected and collectible from taxpayers which is payable to other entities. For example, taxes are collected by the Internal Revenue Service (IRS) for the Social Security Administration.

---

Federal Accounting Standards Advisory Board
Federal Accounting Concepts and Standards
December 31, 1996

## Revenue Standards

Revenue is an inflow of resources that the government demands, earns, or receives by donation. Revenue arises from exchange transactions and nonexchange transactions.

## Exchange Revenue

Exchange revenue is an inflow of resources to a government entity that the entity has earned. It arises from exchange transactions in which each party to the transaction sacrifices value and receives value in return.

Such revenue should be recognized at established prices when services are performed or rendered or when goods from inventory are delivered. For goods made to order or specific services produced to order, the contract price should be recognized as revenue in proportion to the estimated total cost when goods and services are acquired to fulfill the contract. Bad debt expense or revenue reductions should be recognized when it is probable that established prices will not be realized.

Exchange revenue should be recognized in determining the net cost of operations of the reporting entity. The components of the entity's net costs, i.e., the net cost of its suborganizations, programs, and outputs, should separately include the gross cost of providing goods and services, less the exchange revenue earned, and the resulting difference. The components of net cost should also include separately the gross cost of providing goods, services, benefit payments, or grants that did not result in exchange revenue.

Each reporting entity shall disclose (1) differences in pricing policy from the full cost or market pricing guidance provided by OMB and (2) exchange transactions with the public in which prices are set by law or executive order, which are not based on full cost or market price.

## Nonexchange Revenue

Nonexchange revenues arise primarily from exercise of the government's power to demand payments from the public (e.g., taxes, duties, fines, and penalties), but also include donations. Nonexchange revenue should be recognized when a specifically identifiable, legally enforceable claim to resources arises, to the extent that collection is probable and the amount is measurable. Nonexchange revenue should be measured by the collecting entities, of which the IRS is the largest.

For taxes and duties and related fines, penalties, and interest, this should be done in a manner that enables the collecting activities to account for cash collections and refunds paid, as well as the related accrual amounts. The collecting entities should also account for the disposition of the collections to, and the accrued revenue amounts to be recognized by, the general fund of the Treasury and other funds which are entitled to receive dedicated tax collections.

The components of the tax revenue stream, including self-assessments by taxpayers, assessments by the IRS, penalties and interest, tax abatements, and uncollectible amounts written off, should be disclosed by the IRS, as should the cumulative cash collections and refunds by tax year and type of tax. Information about factors affecting collectibility of revenue and time of collection should also be disclosed.

The estimated realizable value of proposed compliance assessments of taxes not yet recognized as revenue should be provided as supplementary information and, if estimable, the realizable value of pre-assessment work in process by the collecting entities. Also provided, if estimable, should be the amount of claims for refunds likely to be paid to taxpayers but not yet recognized as a liability of the government. Although these amounts are not now accrued because of certain limitations, this standard permits them to be accrued when it is possible to do so.

Other accompanying information should include

- a perspective on how the tax burden is shared among classes of individuals and corporations, and

- any available information on the amount of unpaid taxes due from unidentified non-compliant taxpayers, i.e., the so called "tax gap."

Other information presented may also include

- Tax expenditures, such as the amount of tax deductions and tax credits, which may be relevant to an appraisal of the performance of a government program helped by tax expenditures.

- Estimates of other program-related costs that federal laws and regulations impose on state and local governments and on individuals, i.e., the cost of Medicaid to the states.

## Other Financing Sources Standards

Other financing sources are inflows of resources, other than exchange and nonexchange revenues, which increase the net position of a reporting entity. They include appropriations, transfers of assets from other governmental entities, and subsidies. Other financing sources and nonexchange revenues recognized by the entity constitute the entity's financing for its net cost of operations.

## Appropriations

Appropriations are reported as an asset ("funds with Treasury") and as capital ("unexpended appropriations") when made available for apportionment. The amount of appropriations which is later recognized as a financing source for operations shall be the amount used to acquire goods and services and to provide benefits and grants.

## Transfers of Assets

The receiving entity recognizes a transfer of assets to it from another government entity as an additional financing source for operations. Similarly, the transferring entity recognizes the transfer of assets as a decrease in its financing.

| | |
|---|---|
| **Financing Imputed for Cost Subsidies** | Federal entities often receive goods and services from other federal entities without reimbursing the providing entity for all the related costs. This constitutes a subsidized cost to be recognized by the receiving entity. An imputed financing source is recognized to offset any imputed cost required to be recognized. |
| **Budgetary Information** | Summary budgetary information about budgetary resources available, the status of those resources (including obligations incurred during the period), and outlays shall be presented on the basis of budget concepts and definitions prescribed by OMB. This information is also to be provided for major budget accounts as supplemental information. In addition, significant detail concerning budgetary resources, such as the amounts obligated for undelivered orders, should be disclosed. A reconciliation should explain the relationship between obligations incurred by the entity during the period and the entity's net cost of operations. |

## Dedicated Collections

A reporting entity may be responsible for dedicated collections from taxpayers or others, e.g., Social Security taxes. Trust and other special funds within the budget, and other fiduciary funds which may be outside the budget, are established to account for these collections and their disposition. Reporting entities should provide separate financial information about the revenues, costs, assets, and liabilities of the funds administered by them on the basis of recognition requirements determined by law, supplemented by accrual accounting information if different.

The amounts by which trust funds may be over- or under-funded in comparison with the requirements of law, as may be the case for trust funds for excise as well as Social Security taxes, shall be provided as supplementary information if reasonably estimable.

Federal Accounting Standards Advisory Board
Federal Accounting Concepts and Standards
December 31, 1996

# Accounting for Selected Assets and Liabilities

The federal government has financial assets and liabilities for which it must provide proper accounting and reporting. These assets and liabilities include, for example, cash, accounts receivable, advances, and accounts payable. Accounting standards for assets and liabilities such as these are provided in *Statement of Federal Financial Accounting Standards Number 1, Accounting for Selected Assets and Liabilities*.

Standards for additional financial assets and liabilities are provided in statements 2 and 5 on accounting for direct loans and loan guarantees and on liabilities of the federal government.

## Significance of Standard

This standard provides for useful categorizations of assets and liabilities, including categories for those assets which the entity has authority to use in its own operations and those for liabilities not covered by budgetary resources.

Among the financial assets are the entity's fund balance with the Treasury and investments in Treasury securities. The former represent unspent appropriations. The latter represent securitized amounts which eventually will require future receipts to replace trust fund receipts used by the government for current purposes. Federal entities (particularly trust funds) invest excess cash mostly in nonmarketable Treasury securities to meet the government's current cash needs.

Asset valuation guidance provided by the standard will result in recognizing likely losses on federal receivables, such as amounts due from non-compliant taxpayers, when loss conditions are identified.

## Asset Standards

The selected assets for which specific accounting standards are provided are cash, fund balance with Treasury, accounts receivable, interest receivable, advances and prepayments, and investments in Treasury securities. Assets which the entity has authority to use in its own operations should be separated from other assets. These categories should be further subdivided between items arising from transactions with other federal entities and those arising from transactions with non-federal entities.

---

Federal Accounting Standards Advisory Board
Federal Accounting Concepts and Standards
December 31, 1996

| | |
|---|---|
| Cash | Cash on-hand (including imprest funds) or on-deposit and readily negotiable cash instruments held should be recognized as an asset by a federal entity. |
| Fund Balance with Treasury | A federal entity's fund balance with the Treasury is the aggregate amount of funds in the entity's accounts with Treasury for which the entity is authorized to make expenditures and pay liabilities. The fund balance is increased by receiving appropriations and the like; it is reduced by disbursements, investments in U.S. securities, etc. |
| | Disclosures should distinguish the obligated balance not yet disbursed and the unobligated balance. In addition, entities should explain any discrepancies between the fund balance with Treasury in their general ledger accounts and the balance in Treasury's accounts and explain the causes of the discrepancies. |
| Accounts Receivable | A receivable should be recognized when a federal entity establishes a claim to cash or other assets against others, either based on legal provisions, such as a tax assessment, or as a result of goods or services provided. |
| | Losses on receivables should be recognized when it is more likely than not that the receivables will not be totally collected. |
| Interest Receivable | Interest receivable should be recognized for the amount of interest income earned but not received for an accounting period. |
| Advances and Prepayments | Advances and prepayments made by a federal entity should be recorded as assets and reduced when goods or services are received, contract terms are met, progress is made under a contract, or the prepayment term expires. |
| Investments in Treasury Securities | Investments in Treasury securities include nonmarketable par value Treasury securities and market-based and marketable Treasury securities expected to be held to maturity. |
| | Treasury securities should be recognized at their acquisition cost. If the acquisition cost differs from the face (par) value, the security should be recorded at the acquisition cost, which equals the security's face value plus or minus the premium or discount on the investment. For investments in market-based and marketable Treasury securities, the market value of the investment should be disclosed. |
| Liability Standards | The selected liabilities for which specific accounting standards are provided in *Statement of Federal Financial Accounting Standards Number 1* are accounts payable, interest payable, and other current |

liabilities. Liabilities arising from intragovernmental transactions shall be separately reported from those arising from transactions with non-federal entities. Entities should also report the amount of liabilities not covered by budgetary resources.

**Accounts Payable**   Accounts payable are amounts owed by a federal entity for goods and services received, for contract progress under certain contracts, and as a result of rental agreements. When an entity accepts title to goods, whether the goods are delivered or in transit, the entity should recognize a liability for the unpaid amount of the goods.

For facilities or equipment constructed or manufactured by contractors or grantees according to agreements or contract specifications, amounts recorded as payable should be based on an estimate of work completed under the contract or the agreement.

**Interest Payable**   Interest payable is the amount of interest expense incurred and unpaid. Interest incurred results from borrowing funds from Treasury, the Federal Financing Bank, other federal entities, or the public.

**Other Current Liabilities**   Other current liabilities are any unpaid expenses that are accrued and are not recognized in specific categories.

Federal Accounting Standards Advisory Board
Federal Accounting Concepts and Standards
December 31, 1996

# Accounting for Property, Plant, and Equipment

The federal government's investment in property, plant, and equipment (PP&E) exceeds $1 trillion. PP&E are tangible assets that (1) have an estimated useful life of 2 years or more, (2) are not intended for sale in the ordinary course of business, and (3) are intended to be used or available for use by the entity.

*Statement of Federal Financial Accounting Standards Number 6, Accounting for Property, Plant, and Equipment,* includes accounting standards for various PP&E categories. This standard also covers accounting standards related to (1) deferred maintenance on PP&E and (2) the cost of hazardous waste removal, containment, or disposal at sites or facilities the federal government operates or has operated.

## Significance of Standard

This standard separates PP&E into that portion (1) used for, and chargeable to, the cost of government goods and services and (2) acquired for other investment purposes. Separating these costs facilitates analysis of the operating expense and prevents distortion due to large, infrequent purchases.

The former is a relatively small part of total PP&E and includes such assets as government buildings and computers. This PP&E is accounted for on the balance sheet and the depreciation of these assets is included in the entity's operating costs over the useful life of the assets.

The latter consists of several categories of stewardship PP&E--federal mission PP&E, heritage assets, and government-owned land. Investments in these assets are included in the operating costs as a discrete element of cost in the year they are acquired; they are not depreciated. The stewardship assets that result from these investments over the years are not accounted for on the balance sheet, but rather in supplementary stewardship reporting, as discussed in *Statement of Federal Financial Accounting Standards Number 8.* Thus, the accounting standards for stewardship PP&E recognition are consistent with the budgetary treatment for these expenditures.

The standard also addresses PP&E-related costs. For example, the hard-to-measure cost of deferred maintenance of federal properties is to be estimated to the extent possible and disclosed. Cleanup costs of

## PP&E Standards

Accounting standards have been provided for four categories of PP&E: (1) general PP&E, (2) federal mission PP&E, (3) heritage assets, and (4) stewardship land. The Board addressed additional reporting requirements for stewardship PP&E in *Statement of Federal Financial Accounting Standards Number 8, Supplementary Stewardship Reporting*.

## General PP&E

General PP&E consists of items that (1) could be used for alternative purposes, such as by other federal programs, state or local governments, or non-governmental entities, but are used by the federal entity to produce goods or services, or to support the mission of the entity; (2) are used in business-type activities, or (3) are used by entities in activities with costs that can be compared to other entities (e.g., federal hospitals compared with other hospitals).

The acquisition cost of general PP&E should be recognized as an asset. Subsequently, except for land which is a nondepreciable asset, that acquisition cost should be charged to expense through depreciation.

## Federal Mission PP&E

Federal mission PP&E has specific characteristics related to its use and expectations about, and risks associated with, its useful life. These characteristics are described in the standard and include, for example, having no expected nongovernmental alternative uses. Presently, only weapons systems and space exploration equipment are believed to exhibit the characteristics outlined in the standard.

These types of PP&E have been placed in a separate PP&E category because applying depreciation accounting to them would not contribute to measuring the cost of outputs produced or to assessing operating performance in any given accounting period. Also, these assets are developed, used, and retired in a manner that does not lend itself to a systematic and rational assignment of costs to accounting periods and, ultimately, to outputs. Annual expenditures to acquire, replace, or improve federal mission PP&E should be shown as a cost in the period incurred.

## Heritage Assets

Heritage assets include PP&E that have historical or natural significance; cultural, educational, or artistic importance; or significant architectural characteristics. Expenditures to acquire, construct, reconstruct, or improve heritage assets should be reported as a cost in the period incurred.

Not all heritage assets are used solely for heritage purposes--some serve two purposes by providing reminders of our heritage and by being used in day-to-day government operations unrelated to the assets themselves. The cost of renovating, improving, or reconstructing the operating components of heritage assets used in government operations should be included in general PP&E. Following initial construction, any renovation, improvement, or reconstruction costs to facilitate government operations should be capitalized and depreciated over its expected useful life. The cost of renovating or reconstructing the heritage asset that cannot be directly associated with operations should be considered heritage asset costs.

## Stewardship Land

The federal government has vast holdings of land and puts land to various uses. If land is acquired for or in connection with an item of general PP&E, it should be categorized as general PP&E. Other land (e.g., land in the public domain and national park or national forest land) should be excluded from general PP&E and treated as stewardship land. The acquisition cost of stewardship land should be reported as a cost in the period incurred.

## Deferred Maintenance Standard

The deferred maintenance standard requires disclosures related to the condition and the estimated cost to remedy deferred maintenance of PP&E. These disclosures should be made in a footnote but be given prominence by including a reference to this unrecognized cost in the statement of net costs. The deferred maintenance standard applies to all PP&E whether reported on the balance sheet or through supplementary stewardship reporting.

## Cleanup Costs Standard

For cleanup costs associated with operations using general PP&E, probable and measurable cleanup costs should be included in the statement of net costs. The amounts should be allocated to operating periods benefiting from operations of the general PP&E. This allocation should be based on a systematic and rational method, such as allocation to operating periods based on the expected physical capacity of the PP&E and the amount of capacity used each period. In addition, disclosure of the total estimated cost is required.

For cleanup costs associated with stewardship PP&E, probable and measurable cleanup costs should be expensed in the operating period that the stewardship PP&E is placed in service. Simultaneous to recognizing the expense, the related liability for cleanup costs should be recognized.

# Accounting for Inventory and Related Property

Federal government agencies hold and are accountable for several types of tangible property, other than PP&E. This includes property in the following six categories:

- inventory (i.e., items held for sale),
- operating materials and supplies,
- stockpile materials,
- seized and forfeited property,
- foreclosed property, and
- goods held under price support and stabilization programs.

*Statement of Federal Financial Accounting Standards Number 3, Accounting for Inventory and Related Property*, provides accounting standards, valuation methods, and disclosure requirements for these categories of property.

## Significance of Standard

Like general PP&E, this standard calls for inventory and related property, which represents non-monetary resources available to provide future government goods and services, to be recorded on the balance sheet.

Historical cost valuation methods are generally used in accounting for inventory, operating materials and supplies, and stockpile materials and generally reflect the cost of budgetary resources expended when these were purchased. When the property is acquired from others by seizure, forfeiture, or stabilization action, current values are used.

The above categories and additional subcategories of property provided for by the standard will help the Congress, agency managers, and others to better understand the utility of the property and aid them in controlling the assets, identifying amounts that will result in cash inflows from sales, and determining amounts available to deliver future goods and services.

---

Federal Accounting Standards Advisory Board
Federal Accounting Concepts and Standards
December 31, 1996

# Accounting for Inventory and Related Property

## Standards

Accounting standards are provided for the six categories of inventory and related property, as follows.

## Inventory

Inventory is tangible personal property that is held for sale, in the process of production for sale, or to be consumed in the production of goods for sale or in the provision of services for a fee. Subcategories are to be established for (1) inventory held for sale, (2) inventory held in reserve for future sale, (3) excess, obsolete, and unserviceable inventory, and (4) inventory held for repair.

Inventory should be valued in the balance sheet at historical cost, except for excess, obsolete, and unserviceable property, which should be valued at net realizable value. The first-in, first-out; weighted average; or moving average cost flow assumptions should be applied in arriving at historical cost. Provisions were made to permit the use of the latest acquisition cost in accounting for transactions with a revaluation allowance to value inventory. Inventory should be recognized as an asset upon receipt of title or goods. Upon the sale or use in the provision of a service, the related expense should be recognized and the cost of those goods should be removed from inventory and included as a cost in the statement of net costs.

## Operating Materials and Supplies

Operating materials and supplies are tangible personal property to be consumed in normal operations. Subcategories similar to those for inventory should be established for operating materials and supplies.

Operating materials and supplies, like inventory, should be valued on the basis of historical cost. Cost flow assumptions similar to inventories should be used. Operating materials and supplies should be recognized and reported as assets when produced or purchased.

The cost of goods should be removed from operating materials and supplies and reported as an operating expense in the period they are issued to an end user for consumption in normal operations. However, in certain circumstances, user operating materials and supplies may be expensed when purchased.

## Stockpile Materials

Stockpile materials are strategic and critical materials held due to statutory requirements for use in national defense, conservation, or national emergencies. When stockpile materials are authorized to be sold, those materials should be disclosed as stockpile materials held for sale.

Like inventories, stockpile materials should be valued at historical cost and similar cost flow assumptions should be used. Stockpile materials should be recognized as assets and reported when they are produced or purchased. The cost of stockpile materials should be removed from stockpile materials and reported as an operating expense upon disposal or sale.

---

Federal Accounting Standards Advisory Board
Federal Accounting Concepts and Standards
December 31, 1996

**Seized and Forfeited Property**

As a consequence of various laws, certain property is seized by authorized law enforcement agencies. Seized assets are monetary instruments, real property, and tangible personal property of others acquired as a result of these proceedings and in the possession of the custodial agency. The seized assets may subsequently be forfeited to the government through abandonment or administrative or judicial procedures.

Seized and forfeited property should be valued at its market value. Seized monetary instruments should be recognized as seized assets when seized and recognized as revenue when a forfeiture judgment is obtained. Seized property other than monetary instruments should be disclosed in the notes to the financial statements. It should be recognized as an asset upon forfeiture and as revenue upon subsequent sale or disposition.

**Foreclosed Property**

Foreclosed property includes any asset received in satisfaction of a loan receivable or as a result of payment of a claim under a guaranteed or insured loan. Foreclosed property should be recognized as an asset upon foreclosure and valued at net present value for foreclosed property on Credit Reform loans and at the lower of cost or net realizable value for pre-Credit Reform loans.

**Goods Held Under Price Support and Stabilization Programs**

These components should be accounted for as follows.

- Commodities should be recognized as an asset upon surrender of title to the government and valued at the lower of cost or net realizable value.

- Nonrecourse loans, with commodities pledged as collateral, should be recognized as an asset upon issuance and valued at the principal amount of the loan less any allowance for expected losses.

- Agreements to purchase commodities at a given price at the option of the seller should be recognized as a liability if a probable and measurable loss is indicated by the net realizable value of the commodities.

# Accounting for Direct Loans and Loan Guarantees

Because federal credit programs provide interest subsidies and sustain losses caused by defaults on loans made to high-credit-risk segments of the population, the costs of these programs are significant and can be anticipated. The Federal Credit Reform Act of 1990 requires that the expected budgetary costs of these loans be recognized in the budget when direct loans are made or federal loan guarantees are issued.

To provide this recognition and reporting, *Statement of Federal Financial Accounting Standards Number 2, Accounting for Direct Loans and Loan Guarantees*, provides accounting standards for federal direct loans and loan guarantees.

## Significance of Standard

Consistent with the budgetary treatment adopted by the 1990 Act, this standard requires that the costs of loan defaults and interest subsidies of post-1991 loans and loan guarantees be estimated and recorded on a present value basis when the loans are first made or loan guarantees issued. Initial estimates of those costs are to be adjusted based on subsequent experience during the time the loans are outstanding.

As a result, financial accounting information is then available to adjust the initial budgetary estimates. Budget analysts and decision-makers can use this accounting information to compare actual cash flows with projected cash flows and the actual costs of direct loans and loan guarantees with estimated costs.

For credit program managers, information on estimated default losses and related liabilities, when recognized in a timely manner, can be an important tool in evaluating credit program performance. Thus, the information required by this standard can help determine a credit program's overall financial condition, identify its financial needs, and enable program managers to take timely action to reduce costs, control risk, and improve credit program performance.

---

Federal Accounting Standards Advisory Board
Federal Accounting Concepts and Standards
December 31, 1996

## Standards

Federal accounting standards for direct loans obligated and loan guarantees committed after September 30, 1991, contain the following essential requirements.

- Direct loans disbursed and outstanding should be recognized as assets at the present value of their estimated net cash inflows. The difference between the outstanding principal of the loans and the present value of their net cash inflows should be recognized as a subsidy cost allowance.

- For guaranteed loans outstanding, the present value of estimated net cash outflows of the loan guarantees should be recognized as a liability. Disclosure should be made of the face value of guaranteed loans outstanding and the amount guaranteed.

- For direct or guaranteed loans disbursed during a fiscal year, a subsidy expense should be recognized. The amount of the subsidy expense equals the present value of estimated cash outflows over the life of the loans minus the present value of estimated cash inflows. The components of subsidy expense should be recognized separately among interest subsidy costs, default costs, and other costs. Fees should be recognized as a deduction from subsidy costs.

- The subsidy cost allowance for direct loans and the liability for loan guarantees should be reestimated each year, taking into account all factors that may have affected the estimated cash flows. Any adjustment resulting from the reestimates should be recognized as a subsidy expense (or a reduction in subsidy expense).

- When direct loans or loan guarantees are modified, the cost of modification should be recognized at an amount equal to the decrease in the present value of the direct loans or the increase in the present value of the loan guarantee liabilities measured at the time of modification.

- Upon foreclosure of direct or guaranteed loans, the acquired property should be recognized as an asset at the present value of its estimated future net cash inflows.

The standards permit but do not require restating pre-credit reform direct loans and loan guarantees at present value.

# Accounting for Liabilities

*Statement of Federal Financial Accounting Standards Number 5, Accounting for Liabilities of the Federal Government*, establishes accounting standards to recognize, measure, and report liabilities other than the selected liabilities covered in *Statement of Federal Financial Accounting Standards Number 1* and liabilities for loan guarantees covered in *Statement of Federal Financial Accounting Standards Number 2*. It provides general recognition principles for liabilities and more detailed standards for (1) contingencies, (2) capital leases, (3) federal debt, (4) pensions, other retirement benefits, and other postemployment benefits, and (5) insurance and guarantee programs.

### Significance of Standard

This standard requires recognition of liabilities resulting from exchange and nonexchange transactions and from other events that arise under law or are otherwise formally acknowledged. The standard also requires that the future outflow of resources be probable and measurable and, for nonexchange transactions, that the unpaid amounts be due. Thus, federal liabilities will be recognized without regard to whether they are funded by the budget at the time they arise, and the costs related to those liabilities will be recognized on a timely basis.

Under the recognition criteria, only unpaid amounts due as of the reporting date to beneficiaries of entitlement programs are recognized as liabilities. FASAB has considered, but to date has not yet recommended recognition, measurement, or disclosure standards for social insurance programs, such as Social Security and Medicare.

### Standards

The recognition points for liabilities associated with different types of events and transactions are defined as follows.

- Liabilities arising from "exchange" transactions should be recognized when one party receives goods or services in return for a promise to provide money or other resources in the future.

- Liabilities arising from "nonexchange" transactions should be recognized in the amount of any unpaid amounts due as of the reporting date.

# Accounting for Liabilities

- Liabilities arising from a government-related event should be recognized in the period the event occurs, if the future outflow or other sacrifice of resources is probable and measurable, or as soon thereafter as it becomes probable and measurable.

- Liabilities arising from a government-acknowledged event should be recognized when and to the extent that the government formally acknowledges financial responsibility for the event and an exchange or nonexchange transaction has occurred.

More detailed accounting requirements are provided for the following specific liabilities.

## Contingencies

A contingency is an existing condition, situation, or set of circumstances involving uncertainty as to possible gain or loss to an entity that will ultimately be resolved when one or more future events occur or fail to occur. Examples of loss contingencies are collectibility of receivables, pending litigation, and possible claims. When a loss contingency exists, the likelihood that the future event or events will confirm the loss or the incurrence of a liability can range from probable to remote. A contingency should be recognized as a liability when a past transaction or event has occurred, a future outflow or other sacrifice of resources is more likely than not, and the related future outflow or sacrifice of resources is measurable. If measurable within a range of amounts, and no amount within the range is a better estimate than others, then the minimum amount should be recognized.

A contingent liability should be disclosed if any of the conditions for liability recognition are not met and there is a reasonable possibility that a loss or an additional loss may be incurred. Disclosure should include the nature of the contingency and an estimate of the possible liability, an estimate of the range of the possible liability, or a statement that such an estimate cannot be made.

## Capital Leases

In a lease transaction, the lessee should report a liability when one or more of the following capital lease criteria are met: (1) the lease transfers ownership of the property to the lessee by the end of the lease term, (2) the lease contains an option to purchase the leased property at a bargain price, (3) the lease term is equal to or greater than 75 percent of the economic life of the leased property, and (4) the present value of rental and other minimum lease payments equals or exceeds 90 percent of the fair value of the leased property.

The amount to be recorded by the lessee as a liability under a capital lease should be the present value of the rental and other minimum lease payments during the lease term, excluding that portion of the payments representing executory cost to be paid by the lessor.

## Federal Debt

Federal debt is represented by securities issued by the Treasury or other federal entities. It includes debt held by the public (including the Federal

Reserve) and debt held by other federal entities (including trust funds, such as the Social Security trust funds).

Federal debt transactions should be recognized as liabilities when there is an exchange between the involved parties. Fixed-value securities should be valued at their original face (par) values net of any unamortized discount or premium. Variable-value securities should be originally valued and periodically revalued at their current value, on the basis of the regulations or offering language. The related interest costs of the federal debt include the accrued (prorated) share of the nominal interest incurred during the accounting period, the amortization amounts of discount or premium for each accounting period for fixed value securities, and the amount of change in the current value for the accounting period for variable-value securities.

## Pensions, Other Retirement Benefits, and Other Postemployment Benefits

The expense for pensions and other retirement benefits should be recognized at the time the employee's services are rendered. The expense for other postemployment benefits should be recognized by the employer entity when a future outflow or other sacrifice of resources is probable and measurable on the basis of events occurring on or before the reporting date. Any part of that cost unpaid at the end of the period is a liability. The aggregate entry age normal actuarial cost method should be used to calculate the expense and the liability for the pension and other retirement benefits for the administrative entity's financial statements and the expense for the employer entity's financial statements.

## Insurance and Guarantee Programs

All federal insurance and guarantee programs (except for social insurance and loan guarantee programs, which are not covered by this standard) should recognize a liability for unpaid claims incurred resulting from insured events that have occurred as of the reporting date. These claims should include, when appropriate, those not yet reported. Life insurance programs should recognize a liability for future policy benefits in addition to the liability for unpaid claims incurred. Recorded expenses will reflect these liability recognition criteria. All guarantee programs covered by this standard and insurance programs other than life insurance programs should also report as required supplementary stewardship information, the expected losses that are based on the risk inherent in the insurance and guarantee coverage in force.

# Supplementary Stewardship Reporting

The federal government has stewardship reporting responsibility for

- resources entrusted to it, identified as stewardship PP&E, and certain other stewardship investments in human capital, research and development, and property owned by state and local governments, and

- the financial impact of sustaining current government services.

*Statement of Federal Financial Accounting Standards Number 8, Supplementary Stewardship Reporting*, sets forth requirements for special kinds of reporting on these matters.

## Significance of Standard

This standard provides information on expenditures that are peculiarly governmental and have no real private sector equivalent. The results of expenditures for stewardship resources and investments do not meet the criteria for assets that are required to be reported on the balance sheet, nor is a single year expenditure amount generally relevant to annual measurements of program performance. The required stewardship reporting about them should assist in judging the long-term effectiveness of the expenditures.

For physical capital, like weapons systems, resulting from expenditures over time for stewardship PP&E, accountability for what is on hand is established by a combination of financial and nonfinancial data. Establishing accountability with financial data for certain physical capital (like our national parks, which are covered by this standard) is not practical. FASAB has just begun considering accountability requirements for natural resources on federal land. For investments in non-physical capital, like research and development, accountability is established by relating the expenses over a 5-year period to the resulting outputs and outcomes. The off-balance sheet presentation of investments in physical capital facilitates making fair comparisons with investments in non-physical capital.

For the financial impact of sustaining current services, the 6-year forward data provided by the Current Services Assessment provides useful information about the future financial effects of programs such as social insurance and entitlements. This projection of government receipts and expenditures puts programs in perspective and aids evaluation of the sufficiency of future budgetary resources to sustain public services and meet continuing responsibilities.

---

Federal Accounting Standards Advisory Board
Federal Accounting Concepts and Standards
December 31, 1996

The stewardship information presented about resources and investments, together with the information in the financial statements about the government's financial position, when compared with information from previous reporting periods, provides insight on how the government and the nation's financial conditions have changed. The Current Services Assessment assists report users in visualizing how those conditions may change in the future.

## General Requirement

Stewardship information may be presented in varying formats depending on the nature of the federal investments or claims to federal resources controlled by an entity. Such information is required for those entities (1) that control stewardship resources and (2) whose financial statements purport to be in accordance with federal accounting principles and standards, as recommended by FASAB and approved by the Secretary of the Treasury, the Director of OMB, and the Comptroller General. All stewardship information is deemed "required supplemental stewardship information." Audit requirements for required supplemental stewardship information will be established in a collaborative effort by OMB and GAO.

Separate standards for measuring and reporting on specific stewardship elements, extensive discussion, and illustrative material are contained in *Statement of Federal Financial Accounting Standards Number 8*.

## Standards

For supplementary stewardship reporting purposes, information is required for the following categories.

## Stewardship Property, Plant, and Equipment

Stewardship PP&E is property owned by the federal government and meeting one of the following definitions.

- **Heritage assets** are PP&E of historical, natural, cultural, educational, or artistic significance. Heritage assets should be reported in terms of physical units rather than monetary values.

- **Federal mission PP&E** are PP&E integral to certain unique federal missions. Specifically included are weapons systems and space exploration equipment. Federal mission PP&E should be valued and reported using either the historical cost or the latest acquisition cost valuation method.

- **Stewardship land** is land other than that acquired for or in connection with general PP&E. Stewardship land should be reported in terms of physical units rather than monetary values.

Changes in the amounts of stewardship PP&E during the reporting period as well as the balances on hand at the end of the period should be reported. In addition, the condition of the assets should be reported and reference made to the required footnote on deferred maintenance.

## Stewardship Investments

Stewardship reporting should also include data, in nominal dollars, on investments for the current year and the 4 preceding years for the following investment categories.

- **Human capital**, which is costs incurred for education and training programs financed by the federal government that are designed to increase or maintain national economic productive capacity.

- **Research and development**, which is costs incurred for basic and applied research and development efforts to provide future benefits or returns.

- **Nonfederal physical property**, which is grants provided for properties financed by the federal government but owned by the state and local governments.

For human capital and research and development, continued reporting of these items as stewardship investments is predicated on there being output and outcome data consistent with program intent.

## Continuing Responsibilities

Information relevant to the federal government's stewardship responsibilities shall be supplied by furnishing the Current Services Assessment. This is relevant for assessing the sustainability of programs established by current law, that is, the sufficiency of future resources to sustain public services and to meet obligations as they come due. The Current Services Assessment focuses on the totality of government operations rather than on individual programs and provides an analytical perspective on the government because it shows the short- and long-term direction of current programs.

The Current Services Assessment presents receipt and outlay data published in the President's Budget. Data should be presented for all programs for the base year (e.g., the year for which the financial statements are being prepared) and at least 6 years subsequent to the base year, summarized in sufficient detail to identify, at least (1) receipts by major source (e.g., individual income taxes, social insurance taxes, etc.), (2) outlays for the defense, Social Security, Medicare, and net interest functions, (3) all other receipts and outlays, and (4) the deficit or surplus.

---

**Federal Accounting Standards Advisory Board**
**Federal Accounting Concepts and Standards**
December 31, 1996

# Appendix I: Statements of Federal Financial Accounting Concepts and Standards and Their Effective Dates

## Statements of Federal Financial Accounting Concepts

[Effective dates do not apply to Statements of Federal Financial Accounting Concepts.]

*Objectives of Federal Financial Reporting*
(SFFAC 1, September 2, 1993)

*Entity and Display* Effective dates do not apply to Statements of Federal Financial Accounting Concepts.
(SFFAC 2, June 6, 1995)

## Statements of Federal Financial Accounting Standards

*Accounting for Selected Assets and Liabilities*
(SFFAS 1, March 30, 1993, effective for fiscal year 1994)

*Accounting for Direct Loans and Loan Guarantees*
(SFFAS 2, August 23, 1993, effective for fiscal year 1994)

*Accounting for Inventory and Related Property*
(SFFAS 3, October 27, 1993, effective for fiscal year 1994)

*Managerial Cost Accounting Concepts and Standards*
(SFFAS 4, July 31, 1995, effective for fiscal year 1997)

*Accounting for Liabilities of the Federal Government*
(SFFAS 5, December 20, 1995, effective for fiscal year 1997)

*Accounting for Property, Plant, and Equipment*
(SFFAS 6, November 30, 1995, effective for fiscal year 1998)

*Accounting for Revenue and Other Financing Sources*
(SFFAS 7, May 10, 1996, effective for fiscal year 1998)

*Supplementary Stewardship Reporting* [NOTE: This statement is currently before Congress for review. It has been approved by the principals but will not be released as a Statement of Federal Financial Accounting Standards until the review period has been completed.]
(SRAS 8, effective for fiscal year 1998)

---

Federal Accounting Standards Advisory Board
Federal Accounting Concepts and Standards
December 31, 1996

Appendix I

# FASAB Board Members

*Elmer B. Staats, Chairman*

*James L. Blum*

*Philip Calder*

*Donald H. Chapin* (Member through September 30, 1996)

*Martin Ives*

*Norwood Jackson*

*William L. Kendig* (Member through September 30, 1994)

*Edward J. Mazur* (Member through June 30, 1993)

*Gerald Murphy*

*James E. Reid*

*Harold I. Steinberg* (Member through December 9, 1994)

*Cornelius E. Tierney*

*Alvin Tucker*

## FASAB Staff

*Ronald S. Young, Executive Director* (through September 30, 1996)

*Current staff:* Wendy M. Comes (Acting Executive Director), Robert W. Bramlett, Richard L. Fontenrose, M. Lucy Lomax, Richard C. Mayo, Monica R. Valentine, and Richard Wascak. *Former Staff:* Jimmie D. Brown, former Deputy Executive Director, and Frank Rexford.

*In addition to FASAB staff, Board members were supported by the talents and expertise of their individual staff members. Moreover, in the formulation and discussion of the concepts and standards, the Board regularly relied on task forces composed of representatives of federal agency chief and deputy chief financial officers, inspectors general, budget officers, and program managers and on detailees, consultants, and those commenting on the exposure drafts and participating in public hearings.*